World Traveler

Travel to

Nigeria

Matt Doeden

Lerner Publications ◆ Minneapolis

Content consultant: Dr. Abdulai Iddrisu, associate professor of History and African
Studies, Director of Africa and African Diaspora at St. Olaf College

Lerner Publications Company
An imprint of Lerner Publishing Group, Inc.
241 First Avenue North
Minneapolis, MN 55401 USA

For reading levels and more information, look up this title
at www.lernerbooks.com.

Main body text set in Adrianna Regular.
Typeface provided by Chank.

Map illustration on page 29 by Laura K. Westlund.

Library of Congress Cataloging-in-Publication Data

Names: Doeden, Matt, author.
Title: Travel to Nigeria / Matt Doeden.
Description: MInneapolis : Lerner Publications, [2023] I Series: Searchlight books.
    World traveler I Includes bibliographical references and index. I Audience: Ages:
    8–11 I Audience: Grades: 4–6 I Summary: "With over 500 languages and the highest
    population in Africa, Nigeria has become one of the most diverse countries in the
    world. Through engaging maps and images, explore 100,000 years of Nigeria's
    history and culture"— Provided by publisher.
Identifiers: LCCN 2021053155 (print) I LCCN 2021053156
    (ebook) I ISBN 9781728457840 (library binding) I ISBN 9781728463995 (paperback) I
    ISBN 9781728461977 (ebook)
Subjects: LCSH: Nigeria—Juvenile literature.
Classification: LCC DT515.22 .D64 2021 (print) I LCC DT515.22 (ebook) I DDC 966.9—
    dc23/eng/20211214

LC record available at https://lccn.loc.gov/2021053155
LC ebook record available at https://lccn.loc.gov/2021053156

Manufactured in the United States of America
1-50812-50151-6/15/2022

Table of Contents

Chapter 1

GEOGRAPHY AND CLIMATE

From its land to its people, Nigeria is a nation of great diversity. A land of grassy plains, dense jungles, mountains, and deserts, Nigeria is also home to many vibrant cultures and a rich history.

The Land

Nigeria is the world's thirty-second-largest country. It covers 356,669 square miles (923,768 sq. km) of western Africa. Nigeria borders the countries of Benin to the west, Niger to the north, Chad to the northeast, and Cameroon to the southeast. The Gulf of Guinea forms its southern border.

Open plains stretch over much of Nigeria. These include coastal lowlands, deltas, pockets of rain forest in the south, and grasslands and deserts in the north.

Zuma Rock is a large rock hill in central Nigeria once used to defend against invading armies.

These lands have a variety of wildlife, including elephants, hyenas, leopards, and African buffalo.

Highlands rise in the middle of the country. At 7,936 feet (2,419 m) above sea level, the mountain Chappal Waddi is Nigeria's highest peak.

Rivers and Lakes

Two large rivers cut through Nigeria. The Niger and the Benue combine in central Nigeria and flow south to the Niger delta. Silts carried downstream by the river support

Niger River delta

Kainji Dam stretches across the Niger River. The dam creates hydroelectric power.

thick mangrove forests on the coast. The Niger delta is slowly growing as the river deposits more silt every year. Other rivers in Nigeria include the Kaduna, the Anambra, and the Sokoto.

Kainji Lake, Nigeria's largest lake, was made when a dam was put on the Niger River in 1968. Part of Lake Chad lies in eastern Nigeria. Lake Chad, a shallow lake, often changes size depending on the season. Over the past half century, much of the lake has dried up. The lake covers about 580 square miles (1,500 sq. km).

Must-See Stop:
Yankari National Park

It's hard to beat Yankari National Park if you want to see natural beauty in Nigeria. The park, in east-central Nigeria, is built around a series of warm-water springs. After taking a dip in a spring, visitors can see Nigeria's largest herd of elephants as well as lions, hippos, buffalo, and more. A museum offers a look into the region's history as well as threats to Nigeria's wildlife.

Climate

Nigeria has a tropical climate. Temperatures remain warm year round. The southern coastal regions can get as much as 120 inches (305 cm) of rain per year, while the north gets as little as 20 inches (51 cm) per year.

Nigeria has two main seasons, a rainy season and a dry season. During the dry season, a wind called the harmattan blows from the south, through the Sahara Desert, across Nigeria. It often carries clouds of dust lifted from the desert.

RAIN FOREST IN NIGERIA
▼

Chapter 2

HISTORY AND GOVERNMENT

People have been living in what is now Nigeria for a long time. Scientists have found human skeletons that date back ten thousand years or longer. Little is known of these early Nigerian people, but since then a rich history has developed.

Rise of Civilizations

Starting around 1500 BCE, the Nok culture grew in north and central Nigeria. The Nok worked with metal and created huge works of art. The Nok culture thrived until around 200 CE.

Over the centuries, new cultures rose and fell in Nigeria's complex history. The Kanem-Bornu Empire was built on the shores of Lake Chad from around 700 CE to 1300 CE. It traded heavily with distant regions. A group of powerful city-states called the Hausa states became strong trading powers in the 1400s. To the west, the Oyo Empire ruled.

Nigeria's Nok culture created many terracotta sculptures like this one, which was created sometime between 900 BCE and 200 CE.

From British Rule to Independence

In the 1800s, Nigeria became a trading hub where people were captured and sold as forced labor. By the 1820s, Britain had outlawed the trading of enslaved people, but efforts to outlaw it in West Africa didn't take effect until the 1900s. Then people started to trade goods like palm oil for making soap.

In 1900, Britain took control of Nigeria and created the Southern and Northern Nigerian Protectorates. In 1914, the two combined to form the country of Nigeria.

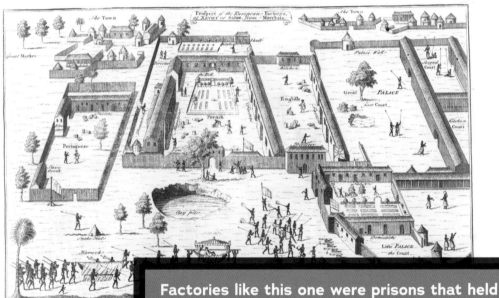

Factories like this one were prisons that held African people who were captured and later enslaved by European traders. Many such factories were built on the Gulf of Guinea.

In October 1960, Nigerian students in London celebrated Nigerian independence.

British rule caused some divisions between the north and the south of Nigeria. In time, more and more people called for Nigeria's independence. On October 1, 1960, Nigeria became a fully independent state.

Struggle and Change

Nigeria is a land filled with many different cultures and religions. Not everyone agreed at first on who should run the country or who should be in charge.

For the next forty years, different groups fought for leadership. The changes in government were hard for Nigeria's people. After many military regimes, in 1999, Nigeria became a democracy again. The new government gave Nigerians a voice in how their country was run. It also provided hope for a more stable and prosperous future.

Traditionally, the Hausa people dress in loose flowing gowns, colorful caps called hula, and turbans.

Let's Celebrate:
Independence Day

Each year, Nigerians celebrate their Independence Day on October 1. The holiday starts with a speech from the president followed by parades and fireworks. Many people wear the colors of the Nigerian flag, green and white. People enjoy traditional cuisine, and some people eat cakes and cookies with green-and-white frosting.

Olusegun Obasanjo was elected president of Nigeria twice, serving from 1976 to 1979 and from 1999 to 2007.

Government

Nigeria has thirty-six states and one capital territory. Each has its own local government. Like the United States, Nigeria has a legislative branch in charge of making laws. The legislative branch includes the House of Representatives and the Senate, an executive branch is in charge of enforcing laws, and a judicial branch applies the law.

Chapter 3

CULTURE AND PEOPLE

Nigeria is called the Giant of Africa. With 219 million people, it's Africa's most populous country. It has a colorful and diverse population, rich in culture, art, and food.

The Hausa are 30 percent of Nigeria's population and live mostly in the north. The Yoruba people make up about 16 percent of Nigeria's population. The Igbo, Fulani, Tiv, and Kanuri make up a combined 25 percent. Many smaller ethnic groups are in the remaining 29 percent.

Religion

Nigerians follow many religions, but Islam and Christianity are the most common. About 53 percent of Nigerians are Muslims. They follow the religion of Islam. North African Berber traders brought the religion to Nigeria more than one thousand years ago. About 46 percent of the population are Christians. Christianity did not become widespread in Nigeria until around the 1800s. Other faiths, such as Bahá'í and Hinduism, have much smaller followings in Nigeria.

Schoolchildren in Lagos dress in traditional Hausa-Fulani clothing to sing Christmas carols.

MOSQUE IN ABUJA

▼

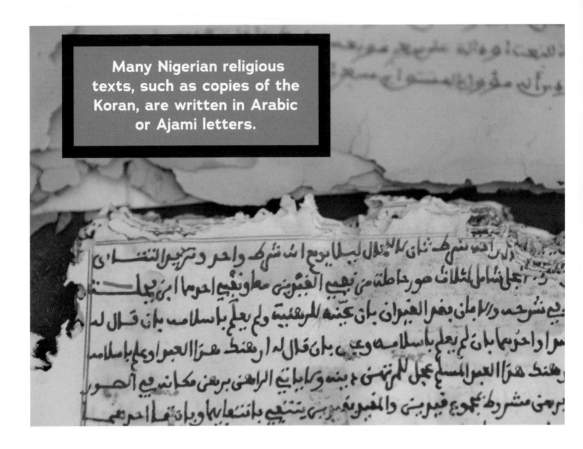

Many Nigerian religious texts, such as copies of the Koran, are written in Arabic or Ajami letters.

Language and Writing

English is Nigeria's official language. Introduced through British colonial rule, it remains the nation's shared language. Many Nigerians also speak native languages. Hausa is the most widely spoken language. It was the official language of Nigeria's northern states until 1967.

Nigeria's languages use various writing systems. Hausa can be written with Latin letters like English or in the Ajami alphabet, which borrows the Arabic letters. In Ajami, letters are formed from right to left.

Must-See Stop:
Nigerian National Museum

Visitors to the Nigerian National Museum in Lagos are in for a treat. The museum displays a wide range of traditional art and Nigerian artifacts. Its Cycle of Life exhibit shows how traditional Nigerians live, from birth to death and even into the afterlife according to their beliefs. Guided tours help visitors get a better understanding of Nigeria's past and present.

Jollof rice is made with long-grain rice, tomatoes, and vegetables.

Food and Art

Nigerian people enjoy a wide variety of cuisine. Rice and beans are the two biggest staples in Nigerian cooking. Beef, goat, and chicken are common meats. Many foods use herbs and spices such as uziza seeds and curry powder. Popular dishes include spicy jollof rice, bean-based Gbegiri soup, and fried plantains.

Nigerian arts and crafts are vibrant and colorful. Artists make detailed leather goods, weave baskets, and create brightly dyed fabrics and clothing. Traditional paintings often feature natural scenes and portraits of Nigerian people.

Chapter 4

LIFE IN NIGERIA

A little more than half of Nigeria's people live in urban areas. Lagos is the largest city, with about 9 million people. Next are Kano (3.6 million), Ibadan (3.6 million), and Kaduna (1.6 million).

Many people in urban areas work in industries such as manufacturing, tourism, health care, and banking. Oil production is a booming business in Nigeria as well. Many of Nigeria's rural population work in agriculture. They farm crops such as corn, cassava, sorghum, and tropical fruit.

Students in Nigeria learn subjects such as math, English language, religion, and agricultural science.

About 40 percent of Nigeria's people live below the poverty line. All Nigerian children are supposed to attend school, but more than ten million do not. Many must stay home to work on farms or do other jobs to earn money instead. Without an education, it is harder for them to find good-paying jobs.

Let's Celebrate:
Calabar Carnival

Each December, the party is on in the Cross River State in southeast Nigeria for the Calabar Carnival. It's called the biggest street party in Africa. It's filled with upbeat music, ornate floats, and parades of people in brightly colored, traditional African clothing. Visitors can sample local foods and dance along to the music in this celebration of Nigerian pride.

Future Challenges

Nigeria is a growing nation, but it faces a lot of challenges. Many of its people do not have access to infrastructure, schools, hospitals, and clean drinking water. This can cause diseases, such as COVID-19, to spread more easily.

Most Nigerians get their water from underground by building hand pump wells.

Desertification is when soil becomes desert because of dry weather or overfarming. Nigeria helps other countries plant trees in a Great Green Wall along the Sahara to stop this process.

Sahara Desert

Conflicts between religious and ethnic groups make life even harder. Meanwhile, climate change is causing more rainfall on the coasts. This threatens Nigerians who live in coastal cities like Lagos. Climate change is also causing droughts inland that make it difficult to grow food.

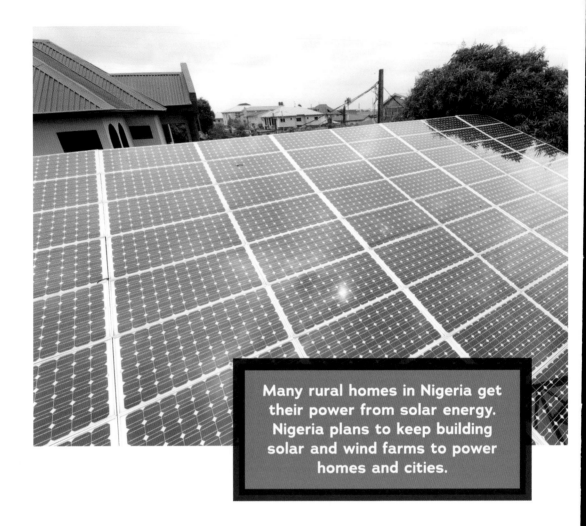

Many rural homes in Nigeria get their power from solar energy. Nigeria plans to keep building solar and wind farms to power homes and cities.

Yet many Nigerians see reasons for hope. In recent years, Nigeria passed new laws to improve access to clean water. Nigeria has also committed to using more renewable energy sources to do their part to slow climate change. Nigerians are working hard to overcome the challenges they face and grow Nigeria into an economic world power.

Map and Key Facts

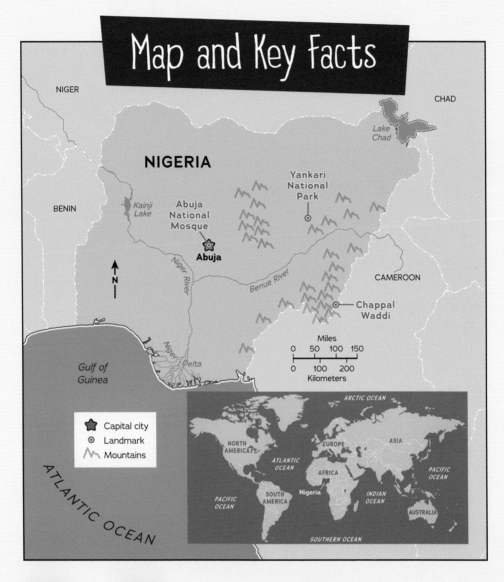

Flag of Nigeria

- Continent: Africa
- Capital city: Abuja
- Population: 219 million
- Languages: English, Hausa, and many other ethnic languages

Glossary

city-state: a state consisting of a city and surrounding territory

delta: a landform created as a river empties into a large body of water

harmattan: a dry, dusty wind that blows over western Africa from about November through March

infrastructure: the system of public structures of a country, state, or region

protectorate: a state that is controlled and defended by another

silt: fine sand, clay, or other materials carried by a river

tropical: a warm, humid climate found near Earth's equator

Learn More

Britannica Kids: Nigeria
https://kids.britannica.com/kids/article/Nigeria/345758

Facts about Nigeria
https://www.kids-world-travel-guide.com/nigeria-facts.html

Hudak, Heather C. *Pathways through Africa*. New York: Crabtree, 2019.

Koontz, Robin. *Learning about Africa*. Minneapolis: Lerner Publications, 2016.

Nanz, Rosie. *Explore Nigeria: 12 Key Facts*. Mankato, MN: 12 Story Library, 2019.

National Geographic Kids: Nigeria
https://kids.nationalgeographic.com/geography/countries/article /nigeria

Index

Photo Acknowledgments

Image credits: Tayvay/Shutterstock, pp. 5, 19; Universal Images Group North America LLC/Alamy Stock Photo, p. 6; Michel Huet/Gamma-Rapho/Getty Images, p. 7; Aminudahiru/Wikimedia Commons (CC BY-SA 4.0), p. 8; Obinna Ibekwe/Shutterstock, p. 9; Werner Forman/Universal Images Group/Getty Images, p. 11; Nathaniel Parr/Library of Congress/LC-USZ62-106828, p. 12; William Vanderson/Fox Photos/Stringer/Getty Images, p. 13; Jorge Fernández/LightRocket/Getty Images, p. 14; Pius Utomi Ekpei/AFP/Stringer/Getty Images, p. 15; Xabiso Mkhabela/Anadolu Agency/Getty Images, p. 16; Olukayode Jaiyeola/NurPhoto/Getty Images, p. 18; Teo Tarras/Shutterstock, p. 20; AP Photo/Jon Gambrell, p. 21; bonchan/Getty Images, p. 22; Emmage/Shutterstock, p. 24; Xinhua/Jiang Xintong/Alamy Stock Photo, p. 25; Oni Abimbola/Shutterstock, p. 26; NASA/Wikimedia Commons, p. 27; Richard J Greenman/Alamy Stock Photo, p. 28; Laura Westlund, p. 29.

Cover: Dr Craig/Shutterstock.com.